COCKATIELS

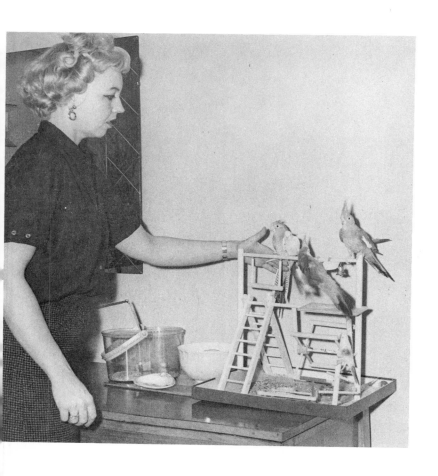

By
NANCY CURTIS

Many of the photos in this book were taken at the Palos Verdes Bird Farm by Mrs. Louise Van der Meid with the assistance of G. Terraneo; others were taken by the photographic staff of Three Lions, Inc.

Cover photo by Harry V. Lacey.

ISBN 0-87666-420-6

Distributed in the U.S.A. by T.F.H. Publications, Inc., 211 West Sylvania Avenue, P.O. Box 27, Neptune City, N.J. 07753; in England by T.F.H. (Gt. Britain) Ltd., 13 Nutley Lane, Reigate, Surrey; in Canada to the book store and library trade by Clarke, Irwin & Company, Clarwin House, 791 St. Clair Avenue West, Toronto 10, Ontario; in Canada to the pet trade by Rolf C. Hagen Ltd., 3225 Sartelon Street, Montreal 382, Quebec; in Southeast Asia by Y.W. Ong, 9 Lorong 36 Geylang, Singapore 14; in Australia and the south Pacific by Pet Imports Pty. Ltd., P.O. Box 149, Brookvale 2100, N.S.W., Australia. Published by T.F.H. Publications, Inc. Ltd., The British Crown Colony of Hong Kong.

TABLE OF CONTENTS

Part of the fascination of Cockatiels is their mischievousness. Here a Cockatiel sneaks some food from a Parrot while the larger bird isn't watching. Photo by Louise Van der Meid at Palos Verdes Bird Farm.

I

The Cockatiel as a Pet

If you are now an owner of a Cockatiel, then there is no need to elaborate to you the joy of owning one of these beautiful, friendly little birds. To those of you who are just purchasing your first "Cockie," may I congratulate you on your new pet, and advise you that you are in for an exciting experience. You no doubt will soon be entranced by the little fellow, and feel as many Cockatiel owners do that "once a Cockie owner, always a Cockie owner."

Just a few of their many fine pet qualities are:
1. They are hardy and easily kept.
2. They are one of the cleanest cage birds available.
3. They require a minimum of time and expense.
4. They are easy to tame, teach to whistle and talk, and to do tricks.
5. They make an attractive and colorful conversation piece and decorator item in any home. Modern and beautiful cages are available in which to house them.

Although the Cockatiel (*Leptolophus hollandicus*) is not yet as popular as the little Parakeet, they are usually readily available in pet shops and through bird dealers. They are relatively inexpensive, both to buy and to keep. They are quite long lived, the average life span being from 10 to 14 years.

These birds are very companionable and get along well with most any other type of bird. They often become quite attached to little Parakeets and are very tolerant of the teasing and antics of the smaller bird.

Cockatiels are among the most affectionate and easily tamed of the smaller Parrot-like birds. Here a Cockatiel is shown with a Halfmoon Conure. Photo by Louise Van der Meid.

The Cockatiel is a naturally friendly bird, but they are excitable and frighten easily. They seem to remember rough handling for a considerable time, despite the fact that authorities claim that birds have no memory. Perhaps, then, it would be best to say that they have an extra keen sense of perception and recall. This would explain why wild birds anticipate the seasons and fly south, and why many birds are able to retain certain whistles and words which they were taught. At any rate, there is not any type of bird or animal which will respond to rough treatment and since Cockies are extra sensitive, great care must be exercised so as not to create any fear in them toward you.

Although the Cockatiel originated in Australia, they are well known in Holland. There has also been much success in breeding and raising them in England, and it was from there that they came to the United States.

The pet Cockatiel, as we know it today, ranges in size from 11 to 14 inches. The wing span can be up to 16 inches. In their natural habitat, they may be much larger. The males appear to have a slimmer body and longer neck. The females, by comparison, have a much shorter, rounder body.

Both males and females dislike any change in their surroundings. This should be remembered when bringing a new bird into your home. If he has been with other birds, he is going to miss his companions and perhaps screech and scream for them. For the first few days, special care should be taken to offset this natural reaction. Keep in mind that, through his eyes, you and your hands are of gigantic proportions. Since he has probably had very little or no handling, the Cockie will be very inclined to bite. For your own protection, as well as to encourage the bird's confidence in you, it is inadvisable to try to handle the bird for the first few days.

If you wish to tame your Cockie immediately, do not place him in a cage with another bird. Even though the other bird is tame, there is absolutely no assurance that your new bird is going to become gentle that much sooner.

Once a Cockatiel learns to know and trust you, you will have a pet and companion that will be well worth every moment of patience and consideration you have extended to him.

The white patch on the wing of this dozing Cockatiel is comparatively broad; on other birds the white area is more narrow. Photo by Louise Van der Meid at Palos Verdes Bird Farm.

2

Coloring of Cockatiels

Until quite recently, there has been little variation in the coloring of the Cockatiel. The body is grey, the back, wings and top of the tail being darker than the breast of the bird. The breast may be a very, very light shade of grey, rather speckled, even appearing to be a "dirty white." There are patches of white on the wing, from a thin streak to three-quarters of the wing. The above description applies to both male and female. The difference in sex is readily apparent on the male, whose head and face are a brilliant yellow. Bordering the yellow, there appears to be a blending of creamy white, particularly around the eye and lower neck. The orange spots appear to be more vibrant in the male, perhaps because of the contrasting yellow. The crest of the male will be yellow near the head and some of these feathers may extend half way the length of the crest. The longer feathers (near the tips) will be grey. The tail of the male is a solid grey, darker than the breast. Looking full front face at the male Cockatiel, his head will appear to be slimmer than that of the female.

The female Cockatiel may have a yellowish tinge to her face, but there will be no sign of the white, as in the male. The orange on the face will appear dull. The feathers in the crest will be either grey or give a drab olive appearance. Because of this, the crest often seems thicker than in the male. The tail of the female, underside, is striped horizontally, grey, black and yellow. In contrast to the male, the head will appear more round, and the neck shorter. These descriptions apply to adult birds only.

Breeders have been trying to achieve an all-yellow or all-white Cocka-tiel. As a result of this, one of the breeders has now been breeding a Pied Cockatiel. This woman has been breeding for a number of years and has sent stock all over the United States. She now has established

There's room in the household for feathered, furred, and finned pets.

Cockatiels get along well with Parakeets, even sharing their play area and food.

strains which she calls "Light Pieds" and "Heavy Pieds." It is possible that some of the Cockatiels on the market today have color characteristics of the Pieds, but they are not prominent. These Pieds are still considered rare and are expensive. It is nearly impossible to determine the sex of these birds except by mating, and owners of pairs do not like to part with them. Should your bird have a few yellow or minute white spots on his body, or appear lighter in some areas (as in a female with a more yellow head) it would not be considered a true Pied. The following is a description of a Pied Cockatiel taken from a copy of a letter sent by a breeder in answer to an inquiry about them:

"*They have a very golden yellow head, against the lemon yellow of the normal male, which both male and female will carry and this color appears in the bird's first plumage and doesn't change with the first moulting. They will have white flight and tail feathers, also white splashes of color on the body, usually on the rump and breast. I call this color white only for lack of a better term as it is actually a cream. In some of the birds, this cream will be quite deep and others it will be lighter in color. These birds are never marked exactly alike, so the description that I am giving is general. The ones I have just described are termed 'Heavy Pieds.' From this strain I get birds that are: normal in appearance, those that carry from a small white spot on the back of the head, some that will have the yellow head only, and then some that have just white flight and tail feathers. This year is the first time I have offered any of these birds for sale. I have been inbreeding this strain in hopes of getting that all-yellow or all-white. In '59 an almost all yellow was hatched; it had four grey feathers across its shoulders. Due to cat trouble this bird was lost, but I have kept it in my freezer to show those who are in doubt that it can be done. I will save this until we hatch another one, which I hope will be this year*". This letter is dated March 10, 1961.

More recently, April 23, 1962, the author received this reply in answer to an inquiry about the Pieds.

"*We do not have any regular Cockatiels for sale at this time, however we do have what we call 'Pied stock,' which we sell. These birds have the same Pied blood line as the Heavy Pieds, but have only small Pied markings on the head or neck. Any pair of these are very likely to throw Heavy Pieds and there is no problem sexing them.*"

The preceding quotations may be of help to those of you who feel that your Cockatiel may not conform to the standard coloring.

Cages for Cockatiels come in many shapes and sizes. Choose the cage which combines beauty and utility.

3
Purchasing Your Cockatiel

Cockatiels are becoming so popular that nearly all pet shops have them, or have access to them. It is always better to choose the bird yourself, rather than have one ordered for you. The exception to this is, of course, when you are ordering a proven mated pair.

Since Cockatiels have definite personalities, and each one may vary, certain traits can sometimes be determined by watching a cage of them. The quieter ones will be eating casually or cleaning their feathers. The more nervous ones will be climbing the bars of the cage, performing various antics for attention, or perhaps their environment disturbs them. Unless the birds have been handled before, the whole

It is all right to put Cockatiels with smaller Parrot-like birds, such as the Parakeet, because the Cockatiel is gentle of nature and will not disturb the smaller birds. But the Cockatiel, for its own protection, should be kept separate from larger birds, like this Cockatoo. Photo by Louise Van der Meid at Palos Verdes Bird Farm.

flock will usually become quite excited and cower in the corner from an extended hand. This is natural, since they will probably have been accustomed to a lot of flight room and much larger quarters. The quieter the bird behaves in his pet shop cage, the more adaptable he will be to the surroundings you bring him to in your home.

The important thing, of course, is to be sure that he is a good healthy bird. If he is missing feathers or "puffed up" and is on the floor of the cage, you should find out all you can about this particular bird, if you are interested in buying him. Plucked feathers in young birds are not uncommon, but his other actions may be indicative of a serious problem. Cockatiels, fortunately, are not easily diseased, but they are quite susceptible to colds and drafts. Frequently a bird catches cold on the way to the pet shop and when placed with a group of other birds, his illness can be easily detected by the puffed up appearance.

Quite often you will see a cage full of Cockatiels, part of which have bands on the leg and the rest will be unbanded. This has nothing to do with the quality of the bird. Banding is merely a record for the breeder. Many good breeders do not band their birds at all. To you, as an owner, the band will mean relatively little, unless you wish to determine the aviary from which your bird came.

A competent sales person may sometimes be helpful in answering your enquiries about the particular bird you have chosen, and you should feel free to ask any questions that you wish before purchasing your bird.

MALE OR FEMALE?

As to buying a male or female, well of course, either one is friendly, both can be taught to talk or whistle (the male seems to pick this up more easily) and both will amuse you with their antics. Once they are tame, they are completely at ease with strangers. The male is the more colorful and perhaps for this reason he is preferred, but the female has a kind of "little girl" sweetness and trustfulness about her that the male has replaced with independence and sometimes a very bold curiosity.

BREEDING PAIRS

If you are buying a pair of birds for mating, then try to determine if they are compatible before bringing them into your home. They usually are, but sometimes one or the other will have been mated

If it is your intention to mate your birds, make sure that you buy a pair that is compatible. These birds get along well together, but not all pairs do. Photo by Louise Van der Meid at Palos Verdes Bird Farm.

before with another mate, and since they are very loyal to their first mates, it may take some time for them to adjust to another. Aside from the times when two males may vie for the attention of a female, this is about the only time there may be problems in the cage. They sometimes grieve for the lost mate for as long as 6 months and during this time appear uninterested in the opposite sex. Their fighting will not be violent, but the feathers will fly. You will have to watch to see that they do not draw blood, for they can continue to pick at an open wound and cause infection. The owner will have to use his own judgment as to whether or not the birds should be separated.

If the birds are separated, the cage doors should be left open. By letting them have their freedom, they soon will visit one another and eat from each other's cage. Finally they will settle on one cage to "set up housekeeping." The writer has found that birds left to their own decisions in this matter settle down more quickly. They are more prolific and compatible than if they were caged together and forced to get along.

There is usually little or no difficulty in putting a Cockatiel with a Parakeet, but caution must be exercised when putting him with larger Parrot-like birds. Because of his placid nature, the Cockatiel may not defend himself and can be bullied and abused to destruction. Here again, it is wise to keep the Cockatiel separate and let him make friends with the other bird himself. His curiosity and anxiety for friends in a new atmosphere will keep him attentive to the other birds, and soon, with his winning ways, he will be welcome with any other type of bird.

Curious and affectionate, Cockatiels are easily tamed to the hand.

4
Determining Age and Sex

Because all young Cockatiels have the feathering of the female until they have their first moult (at about 6 months of age), determining the sex is most difficult. It is highly unlikely that you will get a bird in a pet shop that is less than four months old. At this age they are well adjusted to leaving the nest and capable of feeding themselves. Also any defects or imperfections would have shown themselves at this time.

There are certain characteristics that one can watch for in the younger bird. The feet, for instance, are inclined to have a slightly pinkish tinge. The older the bird, the more scaly and darker grey they are. The beak is lighter (the babies are born with an almost white beak; at maturity it is a dark grey). The body feathers of the younger bird are softer and more fluffy, baby feathers so to speak. If there is not an older bird nearby to make a comparison, determining the texture of the feathers will be difficult, but in most instances, where there are a number of birds combined, there is an obvious difference. Due to the softness of the feathers, the younger bird will appear a little darker on the grey areas of his body. The older bird will be sleek and smooth, and should not be losing any feathers. The babies sometimes are lacking a lot of feather, particularly around the head and neck areas.

Never make the mistake of thinking that the smaller the bird, the younger the bird. Size is no factor, for they do not reach full growth until they are 9 months to one year old. Until that time they grow at various rates.

The length of the crest should be taken into consideration. Mature birds often do not have long crests, and immature birds, or babies, never do. Most Cockie breeders agree that the length of the crest is an hereditary factor, but with proper food and flight room, much has been done to lengthen the crest. At this point the writer should like to point out that both male and female Cockatiels' crests can be exceptionally long, disproving the old story that only the male has the long crest.

The younger bird is easier to handle, for he may not have been previously frightened, but he will not be exceptionally friendly. Unless you want to start handling the bird immediately, there is not too much necessity for insisting on a young bird, for eventually they all become tame with the right kind of treatment and loving care.

As to determining the sex of the bird before the first moult, it is extremely difficult. There have been times when male birds did not moult into their male plummage until they were a year old, leaving the impression until that time that they were females. There have been cases of the females developing yellow near the crest, around the eyes and close to the cere, retaining this coloring until their second moult, then returning to the normal grey head again.

The following is fairly consistent, however: the male bird will nearly always develop (at about age 4 to 6 months) a tinge of yellow around the orange spot, toward the back and sides of his head. The male Cockatiel often develops quite a lot of white or cream coloring on his face. This usually emanates from the orange spot or shows up as a perfect outline around the yellow coloring on his neck.

Cockatiels sometimes lose their underwing feathers first during the first moult. The new feathers of the male are then a solid grey, while in

This young Cockatiel's plumage has developed to the point that the bird will soon attempt to learn to fly. Photo by Louise Van der Meid at Palos Verdes Bird Farm.

the female they are spotted with white. Until the time of this first moult, the underwing feathers are spotted with yellow. The same holds true for the tail, except that instead of spots the feathers are marked with bars.

Although there is not a great deal of difference in the coloring of the eyes between the male and female (each has dark brown) sex can sometimes be determined by the shape of the eye and the location in the head. The female's eye appears to be larger, more almond-shaped, and set farther back in the head. The male often has eyes that are button-round and appear to be set higher in the head and closer together.

A mirror test is often the best way of determining sex when all else still leaves one in doubt. A male bird is far more interested in himself and, when placed in front of a mirror, his vanity will completely overcome him. He talks, whistles, peers and does a little hop that is unmistakably characteristic of these birds. The female may appear attentive to her reflection, but loses interest very quickly.

All Cockatiels, when they are angry or upset, have a tendency to hiss. This also is an indication of fear. The females are much quicker to do this. They also are more inclined to bite.

At this point, I should like to tell you of the time I decided I had an absolutely sure system of determining the sex of young Cockatiels. I had a male Cockatiel which was about three years old. I purchased two young Cockatiels with the understanding that I was to keep the female when I was able to definitely determine the sex. The old male bird took to the two young birds, trying to mate with both of them. I naturally assumed that I was in possession of two young females, and decided to keep both of the birds. Two months later the birds moulted and I discovered I had purchased two males. In mating, it is also a fact, the male birds are consistently the aggressor.

The whistle of the males will range in tone and sounds a little like an off key rendition of "Yankee Doodle." They also tend to sound, at times, as though they are whistling, as you or I might do, for a dog— "whew, whew, whew," ending in kind of a question. The females possess a high shrill shriek, the pitch being a little lower at the end: "eeek, eek, eek."

A veterinarian, or some other such trained person, can sometimes determine the sex by manual exploration of the pelvic area. The bones of the male are pointed and slitted, whereas the female's are rounded and oval.

The removable bottom tray is a most useful feature on this Cockatiel cage. Note that the cage is suitably furnished with toys. Photo by Louise Van der Meid at Palos Verdes Bird Farm.

5
Housing Your Cockatiel

Your Cockatiel's cage should be large enough to allow him to stand straight, flex his wings, and stretch, without touching any part of his body to the cage. A large Parakeet cage is sufficient if you leave the cage door open and allow him daily flights. However, due to his chewing habits (they like paper, lamp shades, matches and cigarette butts)

Some Cockatiels like to take baths and some don't; it all depends on the individual bird. Photo by Louise Van der Meid at Palos Verdes Bird Farm.

it will not do him harm to trim his wings and let him stand on top of his cage, or on a play pen. He will vigorously flap his wings, often hanging head down, and in this way get enough exercise to keep him healthy.

A Cockatiel's feet are larger than a Parakeet's, and thus when the perches begin wearing down after repeated scrapings, they should be replaced. This not only prevents discomfort, but can eliminate a deformity. It is wise to have perches of various sizes in the cage.

Feed dishes should be large enough to hold a good daily supply of seed. They should be stationary enough so that he cannot knock them over, particularly the water cup. The bathing dish should be large enough for him to stand in and deep enough to cover at least half of his body. Once they get used to bathing, Cockies love their baths, and if at first they seem hesitant, a little lettuce floated on the water will increase their interest.

Cockatiels love little toys and will amuse themselves for hours with bells, musical perches, etc. The males especially love mirrors and will talk and whistle incessantly to themselves. The females often become quite devoted and motherly toward the little toys that resemble baby birds.

The cage should be kept in a place where there are no drafts. It should be elevated from the floor. Cockatiels enjoy padding along on a carpet or the floor, but will not stay too long. They are perhaps more aware than we of the drafty condition there.

A cover should be kept completely around the cage at night. Birds do not see well in the dark and often become startled or frightened at strange sounds. They then begin to thrash around in the cage and can injure themselves by catching a wing on the cage bar, or they may spill their water and have to spend the night with dampness permeating the cage, a quick way to catch cold. The cover over the cage acts as an extra measure of security, and the Cockie soon learns that when the cover is on, it is bedtime and he will settle down and remain quiet during the night.

The cage and all seed dishes should be thoroughly cleaned at least once a week. Some dishes may have to be washed daily. A good system of cage cleaning is to put the whole cage in the bathtub, or in a large

Even with freedom of the room to fly in, Cockatiels will usually spend most of their time in a favorite area, thus making it a lot easier to clean up after them.

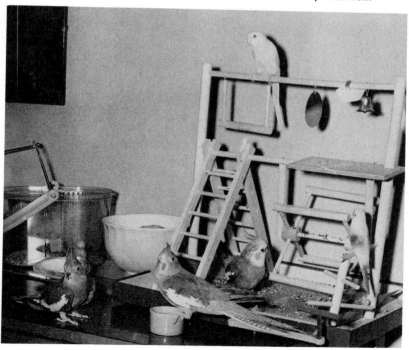

sink, full of water with a germicide. Care should be taken to get into all the cracks and between the bars of the cage where possible mites may be hidden. It is important that the cage be rinsed and completely dry before putting your bird back into it.

The perches should be scraped weekly. Never put damp perches where the birds have access to them. This can cause arthritis. Many pet shops are now offering "trees" which fit in the cage. These are somewhat difficult to clean with a perch brush, so it is wise to have two trees so that they may be scrubbed on alternate weeks, thus giving them a chance to be completely dry. They may also be alternated with perches.

A good commercial gravel paper should be placed on the bottom of the cage. Plain bird cage paper with gravel sprinkled on it will do nicely also. It is a simple matter to remove this paper as needed, thus preventing an excess of droppings from adhering to the bird's feet. Some bird cage papers are available in roll form in a dispensing box. These are very convenient.

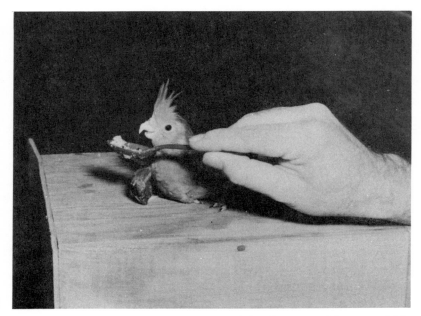

Feeding the bird by hand can be fun for both bird and owner, and is very useful in training. Photo by Louise Van der Meid at Palos Verdes Bird Farm.

6

Feeding Your Cockatiel

The Cockatiel will, if you let him, eat almost anything he can get his beak into. This factor has been pertinent to the death of many of the little fellows. It surely is a joy when he comes to eat from your table or from your lips, but unless this is controlled with moderation, his lust for food can lead to an untimely demise.

The basic daily diet for Cockatiels is Parakeet seed, oats and sunflower seed. Don't forget that the dishes should be clean, and that even the water dish should be rinsed out and replenished every day.

As an addition to a well balanced diet, lettuce, carrot or apple

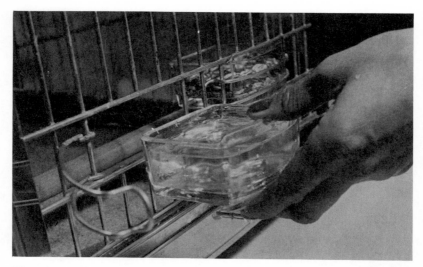

Water in the Cockatiel cage must be changed often, as it is often dirtied by food droppings. Photo by Orlando.

Grit is absolutely necessary to the bird's health; in effect, the grit serves the purpose of grinding up the Cockatiel's food, as the bird has no teeth.

A lining on the bottom of the cage makes removal of discarded food fragments a one-step process. Photo by Orlando.

should be fed twice a week and a small cup of Parakeet treat or millet spray may be kept in the cage. A cuttlebone for calcium is a must, not only for this important mineral, but as an aid to keeping the beak in sturdy condition for cracking the sunflower seeds.

A bird has no teeth and the process of pulverizing and digesting the food is a complicated one. Without gravel, grit, oyster shell or charcoal, or a combination of these, a bird would soon become constipated and die. It is a tragic death to watch. Hence, grit of this kind (there are many on the market) must be kept available at all times. The grit tray is such an integral part of a bird's diet that he is more cautious of keeping it clean than any of his other food.

Any other foods may be very damaging to the system of a bird, although he will be most anxious to try anything, particularly from your lips. If he insists on eating with you, a little whole wheat bread or a piece of fruit will satisfy him completely and act as a nice reward while training.

7
Taming

It does seem that the younger the bird, the easier he is to tame; however, all birds, of all ages, will eventually respond to kindness. The major problem is getting his confidence in you. His fear of new surroundings, lack of companions and strangeness of a new cage are all contributing factors to his wild behavior when you bring him to your home. He will undoubtedly bite when handled, cower in the corner and hiss and strike at your extended hand. Patience is the key word here along with slow, cautious movements. Speak softly each time you approach the cage, and keep the cage near you while you do your chores.

Feed your Cockie at regular hours; they eat well in the morning. Place a full dish of seed in the cage and when he starts to eat, remove it, wait a few moments, then put it back. Place your hands on the cage several times a day and when this no longer excites him, offer a piece of lettuce or apple. As you notice progress being made, try scratching his head very gently with your index finger. He soon will be calling for your attention.

The writer believes it expedites the taming period to clip the wing feathers. Not only will the bird be easier to handle, but in his first flight when you let him out for exercise, he will be less likely to injure himself by flying into walls and mirrors. During this clipping, it would be well to wear gloves, or hold the bird in a heavy towel. If he has not been handled before, such confinement of his body will terrify him, and he may bite. (I don't believe anyone has ever been permanently disabled by a Cockatiel bite, but it can be painful.) Pull the wing out straight as far as possible (you may need some help here). Start clipping nearest the body, following the natural contour of the

Cockatiels can be successfully trained to take food from their owner's lips.

This photo shows how much of the wing feathers must be clipped to hinder the Cockatiel's flying ability.

This is the same Cockatiel, after clipping. Both wings have been treated in the same manner to facilitate taming and restrict flying.

Cockatiels thrive on attention.

wing. The shorter you clip, the less active your bird will be in the air. When he learns that he cannot fly, he will be less likely to try to escape from you. This is a good time to let him ride on your shoulder. A necklace, earring, or some other bright object worn close to the neck area will attract his attention and keep him content and help to ease his fear.

By the time the clipped wing feathers have grown out, your bird should be sufficiently tame to allow him free flight whenever you choose. However, there may be certain high places in your home where you will not want him to perch, and therefore you will want him somewhat limited in his flight. This restriction of flight may be accomplished by pulling out the same wing feathers that were clipped.

The advantage to this is that they grow back quickly and leave no blunt edges (as in clipping) to be caught in cage bars and perhaps broken. When the wings are clipped, the bird will retain the feathers until he moults (every six to eight months). When the feathers are plucked, they grow back approximately every three months.

Wing plucking does not hurt your bird. The longer feathers are grasped firmly, and with one swift tug, pulled completely from the flesh. The shaft of the feather is imbedded in the wing up to $\frac{3}{4}''$ deep. It is important to get all of the shaft, or the feather will not grow in until the next moult. When pulling out the wing feathers, hold the wing with one hand, and pull the feather, in the same angle it grows, with the other.

By using this method, you will be able to control the flight of your bird at all times without marring his beauty or constantly frightening him with scissors.

Leave the cage door open and when he stands on top of the cage, extend your index finger. He may back away to the point where he falls off the cage completely. By continued coaxing he will soon step up onto your finger as though it were a perch. Be persistent, but do not at any time chase him. In his panic, he will become more frightened. Each time he does respond to your finger training, offer the lettuce, apple or special treat.

Let him nibble from your mouth as you do your chores around the house, with him perched on your shoulder. Again, this can be accomplished by placing some bright object in your mouth to get his attention, then replacing it with a treat for him.

There are instances where a bird has been so abused and mistreated that he will grab your fingers and hold on in a painful pinch. If you find yourself in possession of such a bird, wear gloves. When the bird grasps you viciously, hold him under a cold water tap until he releases his bite. Repeat this again and again, until you can extend your hand and he does not grab for you. Usually, one or two sessions will convince him that biting is not proper. Naturally, before placing him back in his cage, you will see that he is reasonably dry, and be extra careful to see that his cage is not near a draft.

It is unwise, at any time, to pick a bird up from the back. They have an intense dislike of having their wings restricted. Finger training is of the utmost importance because of this. Even the tamest of

TROPICAL FISH HOBBYIST

Helping marine, freshwater, and herptile hobbyists for 42 years

Temperate
Marine Fishes

The
Paludarium:
A New
Challenge

Since 1952, *Tropical Fish Hobbyist* has been the source of accurate, up-to-the-minute, and fascinating information on every facet of the aquarium hobby. Join the more than 50,000 devoted readers world-wide who wouldn't miss a single issue.

Subscribe right now so you don't miss a single copy!

After performing satisfactorily, the Cockatiel should be rewarded with a special treat.

birds will bite when they feel they cannot move their wings freely.

Taming a Cockatiel, or any bird for that matter, is a challenge and takes time. It is easy to become discouraged. However, with patience, gentleness and the understanding that to him the human being looks awfully large, it is possible to see daily the bird's confidence grow in you. The reward of the trust, love and devotion he will eventually show are well worth all your efforts.

8

Teaching the Cockatiel to Talk

Both the male and female Cockatiel learn to talk quite proficiently, and although their voices are somewhat shrill, the words they learn are quite distinguishable. The male does much more whistling and can be taught to repeat complete bars of certain tunes. The female is not so adept at this, but she can wolf whistle, and is as quick at learning as the male.

It is almost impossible to teach birds to talk, unless they are in a cage by themselves. Hence, step number 1 is to isolate the bird. He must not be distracted by any of his toys or mirrors or other objects in the cage, and they should be removed. The room in which you work with him should be quiet and free from confusion. All his attention should be directed at you. As an extra assurance of this, place a covering over the top and sides of the cage, leaving only the side facing you open.

For the most part, birds hear through vibrations, rather than through sounds. Therefore, your voice should be as highly pitched as possible. To begin with, you should try to teach him only the words that end with vowel sounds—*hello, pretty, bye bye*, etc. Repeat these words or others of your choice, one at a time, over and over, or whistle the same tune repeatedly. You will notice that your bird will be watching you intently. He may try to imitate you immediately, but do not become discouraged if he does not. Do not try to teach him too large a vocabulary in the beginning, but concentrate on one or two words at each session.

The length of these lessons should not exceed 15 minutes, for your bird may lose interest and completely ignore you. After each lesson, a bit of his favorite treat should be given to him.

Don't attempt to teach your Cockatiel to talk until after he has been tamed.

Make sure that you play with and inspect your birds regularly.

Any time you are near the cage, or feeding or cleaning the bird, repeat the words you are trying to teach him, and always try to maintain the same level of pitch and tone of your voice. Cooperation by other members of your family to do this helps also.

Unless it is unavoidable, the bird should be kept isolated from other birds until he has learned to talk. When they talk among themselves, they are less interested in what you wish to teach them. Once they learn words, even if they are not coached regularly, they do not forget them.

When your bird has learned one word, go on to the next one. Each time he says a word he knows, reward him with his favorite treat or a scratch on the head. Once he has gotten the idea, you can try coupling words, later graduating to sentences.

The first words are the most difficult, but with patience and perseverance, you can have a talking bird. The secret is in working with the bird daily, maintaining the same pitch to your voice, and working with him in conditions where you have his undivided attention.

Harmonious Cockatiel couples are a study in serenity and devotion. Photo by Louise Van der Meid at Palos Verdes Bird Farm.

9
Breeding Cockatiels

Breeding Cockatiels in an aviary, where there is plenty of dirt, sunshine, fresh air and flight room is relatively simple. With a good diet, large nest boxes, and conditions as near to their natural habitat as possible, they settle down with their mates and nature does the rest.

A male Cockatiel inside a typical nest box. Notice the size of the entrance and the position of the perch.

However, when the birds are confined to a small cage, provided only with commercial seed, subject only to room temperatures, the situation is radically changed. In fact, it may be more than difficult to get a pair on the nest.

The first step is to get them into excellent condition for breeding. This means enriching their diet with foods not normally supplied, and you will note that these foods are all mineral enriched. I have found the following mixture to be the most beneficial in getting birds in breeding condition. This will last one pair about a week.

$\frac{1}{4}$ cup Parakeet seed

$\frac{1}{2}$ cup commercial nesting food

$\frac{1}{3}$ cup oats

$\frac{1}{4}$ cup condition food

Mix this together and feed in one container. Add about four full drops of wheat germ oil over the amount placed in the feeding dish. The regular amount of sunflower seeds should be fed separately in another dish.

Plenty of cuttlebone, calcium block, oyster shell and grit should be available, the latter two items in large quantities and changed daily. Lettuce and carrot should be fed daily to keep the bowels loose. If they appear constipated, a little lime water (2 or 3 drops) added to their drinking water will remedy this. A piece of whole wheat bread, soaked in water and dotted with wheat germ oil, will also be an aid in breeding.

Birds raised in outside aviaries are inclined to breed in the spring and fall, but it is not uncommon to find them breeding all year round. Consequently, house birds, unaccustomed to radical temperature changes, may be bred at any time. There is less danger of egg binding when the birds are bred indoors in the winter. However, in the summer they are more subject to mites and this discomfort may cause them to break the eggs while scratching themselves. They may become too warm in the nest box and desert the eggs. The breeder must use his own judgment to prevent this if he plans to breed at this time.

This photo shows the comparative sizes of a chicken's egg (left) and a Cockatiel's egg.

41

The aforementioned diet is extremely rich and caution must be exercised to see that the birds do not get overly fat. There is but one remedy for this, and perhaps it is the most important of all: THE BIRDS SHOULD BE GIVEN ALL THE EXERCISE AND FLIGHT ROOM POSSIBLE. They must feel as free as though they were in their native woods. The cage door should be left open at all times. If you are fussy about your furniture, or are not around to clean up after them, better not try breeding in the house. They are messy, but only at this time, when chewing and activity is so important.

A nest box should be placed as near to the cage as possible, on top, or at least where, when they are flying, they can both view it. With their freedom, nest box, and the enriched diet, you will note that the

A scooped-out dish is not always necessary, for many times the eggs are laid on the bare floor if the nest box is large enough.

The parent birds often spend time in the nest box together.

copulation period is longer. At this time, a check should be made of the vents of both birds, to insure that there are no overgrown feathers that may interfere with the mating.

THE NEST BOX

The nest box should be wooden and have a partition in the middle to keep the eggs from rolling too much. It should be large; this is stressed for two reasons:

1. Both birds incubate the eggs and spend hours together in the box. They need room to move freely and turn the eggs.
2. The nest box will act as "nursery" for the chicks until they are old enough to leave it.

The box should have a $3\frac{1}{2}$ inch hole in the center and a perch outside to make access easier. In fact, everything should be done to make

A soft-shelled egg like the one shown here is often the result of improper feeding. Without the necessary minerals, especially calcium, in the diet, the female can not meet the demands made on her body by the developing eggs. Photo by Louise Van der Meid at Palos Verdes Bird Farm.

Newly hatched Cockatiels are helpless and need constant attention. Photo by Louise Van der Meid at Palos Verdes Bird Farm.

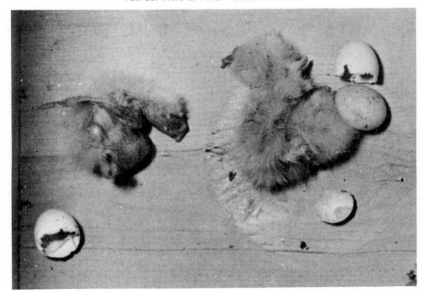

the nest box convenient and easily accessible. The female is especially cautious at this time. There must be no fear of entering or leaving it. If the box is too small and they both try to get inside, they may step on the eggs or roll them together and break them. They can be patched, either with clear fingernail polish or a piece of another egg, but usually by the time the damage is discovered, part of the fluid has been lost and the egg is useless. IT IS IMPORTANT TO HAVE A LARGE NEST BOX, the ideal size being at least 16″ × 16″. The partition should mark off about half this area.

As soon as the nest box is placed in the cage, both birds will investigate, and begin scratching and chewing on it. It is necessary for

A young Cockatiel peeks out from the nest box. Photo by Louise Van der Meid at Palos Verdes Bird Farm.

the breeder to help them with material to lay the eggs on. Shavings, Pablum or some other soft material (but never cotton or cloth) should be placed about 1 inch deep on the floor. They will arrange this to their liking.

Copulation between the male and female continues right up until the time the egg is laid. However, two or three days before the first egg is laid, the female exhibits obvious signs of her pregnancy. There is a lump on the underside of her tail near the vent. Although the male continues with his lovemaking, and during the actual act of copulation will take longer, the female seems uninterested. Her tail feathers will become ragged from spending so much time in the box and arranging the material for the eggs. She often appears puffed up and she ruffles herself regularly. She assumes a more bloated and "hunched" position on the perch. Her breathing appears to rack her whole body.

During the entire nesting period she continues her normal pattern of bathing, often coming out of the nest box twice a day to bathe. The bath water should be at least room temperature as a guard against chilling and egg binding. She does this to keep the eggs moist.

On the days the eggs are laid, both birds will stay in the nest box together. At times one or the other will come out to eat. The female always visits the grit tray and calcium block. This procedure continues during the entire incubation period. Their schedule is so arranged that after all the eggs are laid, the male spends nearly all day on the eggs, and the female eats, bathes and enjoys flight and freedom. She will on occasion relieve him to eat and drink, and will sometimes sit with him, at which time they share the eggs. At night, however, the female sits and the male stands outside the box or locates himself very near the cage or nest box entrance.

A clutch of eggs varies from 4 to 8. The more eggs, the closer the female must be watched. With each egg she labors, sometimes the labor lasting as long as 10 hours. Her breathing becomes heavier, she appears more tired, and there will be a spasmodic twitching of the tail. At the actual time the egg is laid, she will back into a corner, her tail is propped on the side of the box and her head nearly rests on the floor. Here she strains for up to an hour. As soon as the egg is laid, she rolls it with her beak to the center of the box. Then she tucks it gently under her breast and the incubation begins. During the egg-laying process, the male sits on the already laid eggs. He continues to stay with her until she is rested and capable of setting on the whole clutch. The turning of the eggs is done, as described above. This is mostly done by the female and it is with genuine loving and gentle care that she rolls and turns the eggs, then once again tucks them carefully under her breast.

It would be reasonably accurate to say that the eggs are laid about every 48 to 52 hours—that is, every other day. Unless it is absolutely necessary, it is not wise to disturb the nest. Despite the fact that

Hand feeding is one of the greatest aids to the Cockatiel owner in taming the bird. Once the Cockatiel's trust is won, the job is half over. Photo by Louise Van der Meid at Palos Verdes Bird Farm.

removing the eggs as they are laid, and replacing them with plastic eggs—returning the full clutch when the egg laying period is finished —will contribute to hatching the babies all at the same time, rather than every other day as they should, this procedure will keep the hen on the nest for at least another week. She may get tired and desert the nest before the incubation period is completed. When all the chicks hatch at once, this exerts a greater problem for feeding on the parents and they may neglect them completely. Instinct has a way of knowing when nature has been tampered with, and no matter how faithful to the eggs the mother is, these factors may contribute to her leaving the nest before the eggs have hatched, or before the chicks are capable of caring for themselves. Unless you have access to a commercial incubator, the eggs are best left strictly to the parents' care.

During the last days of incubation, the eggs to be hatched first will be left to one side for a period of time each day. This may be to allow the chick to cool inside the shell, thus preparing it for its hatching. Also during the latter part of the incubation period of those eggs that have not yet hatched, the male spends more time in the nest box and often cares for the chicks at night, while the female sets on the remaining eggs.

On the 18th or 19th day after the egg has been laid, a tiny hole appears in the side of the egg. At this time the chick can be heard chipping at the shell and making his very first "chirps." Just a matter of hours later, the chick emerges from the shell. The parents clean the baby, for there is a kind of afterbirth encrusted on his body. Shortly thereafter they will feed the little one by regurgitating food into its mouth. It is best to leave the chicks with the parents for a few days. They do seem to get a better start by doing this.

At times the parents do not feed the chicks, and they must be hand fed. The main reason the parent birds do not feed the chicks is that they have not been provided with proper food. A mixture of equal parts of nesting food, Pablum and strained bananas should be moistened with water and placed in the cage a week before the eggs are to hatch. Again, add two drops of wheat germ oil to this mixture.

Should the chick be stuck in the shell due to insufficient moisture (again the importance of available bathing facilities for the parents) the pair will throw the egg from the nest. These discarded eggs should be removed. Once the birds begin eating and picking at the eggs, they can never be trusted again and may try to destroy other eggs, even though their original intention was to help free the chick. Once the eggs have been discarded or abused by the parents, there is little one can do to save the unborn chick. The egg may be rubbed with a moistened cloth and incubated with a light bulb, but the chances are slim that the egg will hatch.

During the entire incubation period, the parents keep the nest box spotlessly clean. They contain all their droppings within themselves until they are well away from the nest box. Because of this, it may be alarming to the novice breeder to note the size and color of the droppings, which are large, loose and a lighter shade of green. There is also a considerable amount of white, due to the excess intake of gravel and calcium. If the droppings are actually runny, the bowels can be tightened by lessening the amount of lettuce or lime water. However, at this time the birds should not become constipated and it is safer for the bowels to be a little loose.

Before beginning the breeding period, the birds should be examined closely for mites, and if during the incubation period they are suspected, the birds should be sprayed with a good mite spray. This can be done while they are outside the nest box (so as not to damage the eggs). A preventive measure can be taken by spraying the nest box when setting it up, as well as the cage. Both cage and nest box should

Already hungry, these baby Cockatiels scrabble around in their nest box, looking for food. Photo by Louise Van der Meid at Palos Verdes Bird Farm.

be well cleaned before starting, for aside from cleaning the bottom of the nest after the babies are hatched, it is difficult to clean the cage while the parents are nesting.

Birds begin mating very early, but very rarely breed before they are one year old. Once they pair up, they are faithful to one another, and will grieve if separated. Often, when separated from her original mate, a hen will never lay eggs again, although she will permit mating.

As soon as the chicks are ready to leave the nest, at about 5 weeks of age, the pair may be willing to nest again. To prevent this, for the strain of such close breeding is unhealthy, the nest box must be removed from the cage. It may be necessary to separate the birds entirely, but usually removing the nest box and cutting down on the breeding foods is sufficient to discourage them. There is less need for full time exercise, and they may be confined for part of the day. Two clutches of eggs a year are enough for these birds. They do need time to rebuild and vitalize their systems. Although there have been cases of breeding up to four times a year, the full clutch did not hatch, the chicks were weak, and the parents became listless, tired, and their life span was considerably shortened.

Sometimes Cockatiels will not begin to incubate the eggs until there are at least two in the nest. If, after that time, it does not appear that they are going to remain in the nest, place a piece of wood, cardboard, cuttlebone or some other favorite chewing material in the box. They then may amuse themselves while setting on the eggs. It is not wise nor helpful to pen them in the box. They may try to destroy the eggs. Keep a watch that they have enough calcium and wheat germ oil and give them all the privacy you can.

In the event that any of the eggs do become broken and the fluid drains out before it can be patched, these eggs should be removed. Again, the parents may try to clean the egg, further breaking it. As mentioned before, once they acquire a taste for the eggs, they can never be trusted again.

It has been stressed that privacy and avoiding contact with the birds on the nest is all important. You may then wonder how you will know if all is well inside the box. You will know by the absolute routine way in which their setting is conducted. Any quarrelling excitement, or the sight of both birds off the nest at the same time, is an indication of trouble.

There are many reasons why birds mate but do not have eggs. As indicated earlier, they do not take easily to a new spouse if they have been mated before. They may be too young (attempted breeding should not take place before they are one year to 18 months old). Improper diet is a factor. If none of these causes seems likely, then it is recommended that a veterinarian examine your birds, for the causes may be internal.

It should be noted here that your birds should be accustomed to their present surroundings. They must be well adjusted to their home, their feeding and cleaning schedule and their handlers. The less flighty and nervous they are, the better your chances for successful breeding and healthy chicks. Therefore, the last requisite is patience.

Without a good mineral-rich diet, the female may produce soft-shelled eggs, and the male may be incapable of fertilization. Photo by Louise Van der Meid at Palos Verdes Bird Farm.

10

Infertile Eggs

It is difficult to pinpoint the causes of infertile eggs. However, a diet supplied with all the necessary minerals that a cage bird normally lacks is a pertinent factor. Although both birds play an equal part in achieving fertility, the writer believes that the female is more important here. Without calcium, grit and wheat germ oil the eggs may be soft shelled, in which case they rarely hatch. If she is nervous she may become eggbound. If she is flighty she will not nest. The male, on the other hand, requires a good diet, but has far less responsibility as far as the eggs are concerned. A poor contact between the male and female during copulation can prevent fertility also. It has been mentioned earlier the importance of trimming the vent feathers.

Any drastic change in housing may upset the birds enough to cause infertility. Their systems are so delicate and they are so averse to changes in their routine that they may go through a period of sterility.

Handling the eggs is dangerous, although after one week it is less so. However, body heat from the hand or moisture that is absorbed through the shell in the early stages of incubation may cause the egg to become infertile.

Loud noises, such as thunder, hammering, etc., can cause the death of an unborn chick. If there is a lot of confusion and fussing around the nest box, this can be fatal, especially if the box is moved or jarred in any way.

As with any egg, the Cockatiel egg is fragile and for successful hatching should be treated and guarded as attentively as a jewel. The eggs should be left in the nest a full 21 days before being discarded as infertile.

Ugly to the point of being grotesque, these babies will soon develop into beautiful birds. Photo by Louise Van der Meid at Palos Verdes Bird Farm.

II
The Babies

When the babies are first hatched, they are far from a beautiful sight, except perhaps to the owner who has waited long and patiently for their arrival. The head and neck are the largest part of their bodies, and their eyes, not open, almost cover each side of the head. The amount of feathers on the body varies. Some of them have a few straggly olive colored quills, while others are covered with a brilliant yellow down. They are very active and appear to be walking around on four legs, since they use their wings for support. They are born hungry and crying for food. Within two hours after hatching, the parents will be feeding them. The male does the largest part of the feeding. The value of having softer foods available to the parents is again stressed here. They will already have become accustomed to it and seem to know that it belongs to the baby. The regurgitation is that much simpler.

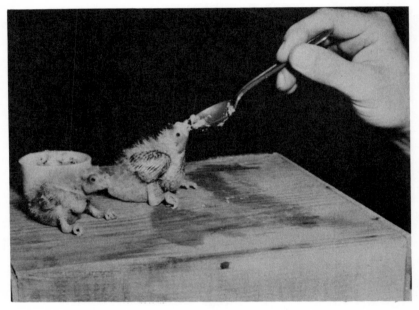

Hand feeding at a very early age makes taming easier later on. Photo by Louise Van der Meid at Palos Verdes Bird Farm.

If the babies are left to the parents to feed, they must be watched for the first few days. The parent birds often regurgitate the food onto the baby's back, re-eat it, and feed the baby. This regurgitated food, when left on the baby, becomes sticky. The parents will then try to clean the baby, and in their efforts can injure or kill it. The baby should be wiped off carefully with a piece of cotton and warm water, dried thoroughly and placed back in the nest box after each feeding, if this condition exists. One will easily recognize the sound of the feeding, and the crop will be full. Listening and watching for these signs will tell you when the bath is needed. The food also has a tendency to accumulate around the beak. To avoid sores in this area, do include this in the bath.

The parents keep constant guard on the nest box until the babies are about five days old. At this time they will leave the nest box together. The owner can then handle the babies and begin supplementing their diet with a few drops of vitamins and warm water daily. Naturally, they should not be handled any more than necessary, and during all the times they are out of the nest box, they should be kept warm. It simplifies the handling to use a gauze pad or square of cotton.

The babies open their eyes when they are about 8 to 10 days old. If they have been bathed properly, there should be no problem. On occasion, however, the eyes do become stuck. Repeated washing with boric acid in warm water, and a close watch to see that the parents

Young Cockatiel perches atop nest box. In their younger stages, Cockatiels are less curious and do less exploring. Photo by Louise Van der Meid at Palos Verdes Bird Farm.

do not try to pick at them, should remedy this.

At about five weeks of age, the babies will be completely feathered out. The body will be almost as large as the parents. They then begin to leave the nest and pick at the food in the cage. The food should be sprinkled on the floor of the cage until they learn from the parents about seed cups. When the owner is sure that the chicks are completely capable of feeding themselves, they may be removed from the nest box to a separate cage. The parents may still continue to attempt to feed them until they are about 7 weeks old. The sooner they achieve their independence, the better it is for both parents and chicks.

HANDFEEDING

Handfeeding can begin any time after the chicks are hatched, but it is a difficult and tedious process when the chicks are less than three days old. After this time, they are a little easier to handle.

Rewarding the Cockatiel with tidbits helps in taming the bird. Despite its powerful beak, the Cockatiel will rarely nip its owner while taking food from its owner's lips.

Feeding can be done with an eyedropper. At first, only a small amount of food is necessary to fill the tiny crop. Each day, however, a little more food will be consumed. If the chick is constantly hungry, the consistency of the food may be increased to make it more filling. For those first crucial days, a two hour feeding schedule should be maintained. Night feedings can be lengthened to every four hours. The breeder must use his judgment as to the length of time between feedings. The crop is a good gauge and should never be completely empty.

An excellent diet to handfeed baby Cockies follows:

Mashed, strained bananas—the type used for infants.

Pablum—enough to thicken to proper consistency.

A pinch of nesting food—pulverized if possible.

Once a day, vitamins or wheat germ oil should be added to this.

The food should be at least body temperature.

This mixture should never be prepared more than 12 hours in advance.

After the chick has his eyes open, this mixture can be fed from a spoon. A small dish of this food should be kept near them at all times. Water, in a large, unspillable dish must also be kept near them. A little gravel, Parakeet seed and nesting food should be sprinkled on the bottom of their box. Until they are old enough to crack and eat them, sunflower seeds are great toys for them and they proudly carry them around in their beaks. At least daily, more often if necessary, the bottom of the box should be cleaned and lined. Do be sure that none of the soft food mixture solidifies to the baby's body. They will try to pick at it, causing difficult-to-heal sores.

At about the age of 6 weeks, the handfeedings can be cut down to twice a day. Some chicks do not require handfeeding for this long. Here again, the breeder must use his judgment. It is a good policy to always check the chicks at night, and perhaps that will be the only time they will need to be handfed.

Although it is said that handfed chicks make tamer adult birds, if the chicks are handled periodically from their infancy, they show no fear. They often are just as tame as the handfed ones.

This bird is suffering from a condition similar to French moult. This is in many cases a congenital condition. Photo by Louise Van der Meid at Palos Verdes Bird Farm.

12

Illness

One would have to have a complete medical background to go into the history, nature and causes of all bird diseases. However, our purpose here is to advise you, the pet owner, of certain signs of illness and home remedies that may be used in their event.

Cleanliness is, of course, the prime requisite of a healthy bird. A good mite spray when needed, frequent baths and fresh, clean seed are of the utmost importance.

COLDS

The bird will remain listlessly in one position in the cage. The feathers will be puffed up. Appetite is poor, droppings abnormal. Remove the bird to an isolated cage. Place a cover around it so that he will remain quiet. Place only the smaller seeds (Parakeet and oats) in his cage. A pinch of Sal Hepatica in the drinking water will clean the bowels. (This may be administered directly with an eye dropper twice daily.) When the droppings appear normal, the regular diet may be restored. Be sure that the bird has cuttlebone and gravel at his disposal at all times. Keep him isolated until droppings, diet and actions are entirely normal.

CONSTIPATION

The bird will hang on the sides of the cage, or on a perch in a cramped position. Droppings will be tight, dark green and dry. Isolate the bird and follow through with the Sal Hepatica as described above. A soft diet of mashed banana, lettuce, and whole wheat bread soaked in water and sprinkled with wheat germ oil should be the only food until the appetite returns to normal. As this occurs, replace the regular diet. Droppings usually return to normal within two days.

EGGBOUND

The hen will remain in a cramped, head down position. Her body will spasmodically expand and contract as she labors over the egg. Gently remove her from the present cage or nest. Place her in a lined box, and administer heat to the bottom of the box. One must be careful not to overheat. If the hen is tame enough to handle, a little mineral oil should be given by eye dropper. Water should be the only food in the box, although she may nibble on a piece of lettuce. The top of the box should be left open. At this time, if she wishes to walk or exercise, it will be to her best interest. As soon as the egg has been dropped, return her to the nesting cage so that she may eat. The egg should be handled with tissue or cotton and placed with the rest of the clutch, or in the nest box site they have chosen.

MOULTING

Cockatiels have their first moult at 5 to 6 months of age. After that, they moult every 8 to 12 months; during moulting, their resistance is lower and they are more susceptible to colds and drafts. A small amount of moulting food may be mixed with their regular seed. This food has egg in it, and the writer does not advocate its prolonged use. Discontinue the use of the moulting food as soon as the bird has completed the moult. The moulting period lasts from 2 weeks to a month.

ALBUMIN POISONING

This condition is first noted by an excess of yellowish fluid in the droppings. The bird becomes emaciated almost overnight and cannot even elevate himself to a perch. The two main causes for this condition are: (1) too much egg food, and (2) old, mildewed seed. As in other instances, the bird must be isolated and kept warm. The only food given to him should be Parakeet seed, with extra millet added. The seed should be first dusted by shaking it in a piece of gauze. Water and gravel should be kept in the cage at all times. This disease is nearly always fatal, but if caught in time, death sometimes can be prevented. The bird should never again be fed egg food—even the slightest amount can trigger this illness. The bird never really regains complete health. Handfeeding of mashed bananas and Pablum is recommended if the bird is in too critical condition to eat by himself. The recovery period is, if effected, one to two weeks.

STUNNING

It is not unusual for a bird, in strange surroundings or in fright, to fly into a wall or mirror and render himself unconscious. When this occurs, wrap him in a washcloth and apply cold compresses to the head and neck. Be sure to dry him off as soon as he recovers. Keep him caged until his wings are clipped sufficiently so that he cannot fly with such force.

BROKEN BONES

Broken bones should be treated only by a competent veterinarian. The amateur may permanently disable the bird by incorrectly trying to set a splint.

OPEN SORES AND WOUNDS

There are commercial salves on the market that are excellent for treating these wounds. They may be applied with a piece of cotton. Until such time as these salves may be purchased, or for cracked, parched feet and beaks, Vaseline applied sparingly to these areas may be used. The bird should be isolated from others. If he persists in picking at his wounds, it may be necessary to bandage with gauze.

EYE AND NOSTRIL INFECTION

After a cold, the eyes and nostrils sometimes become congested with mucous matter. This should be cleaned three or four times a day with a boric acid solution and warm water applied with cotton. After each application, the area should be wiped dry with more cotton.

ADMINISTERING TO THE SICK BIRD

In cases where the bird is too ill to eat by himself, he should be hand fed. A soft diet is best, consisting of mashed bananas and nesting food, with a little Pablum to mix to the right consistency.

The bird should be held firmly in the left hand, with the head between the thumb and index finger. With the eye dropper in the right hand, place the tip of the dropper on top of the bird's tongue, as far back in the throat as possible. After each administration, release the bird so that he may swallow and get it into his crop without choking. Repeat the process until you get a sufficient amount of food or medicine into the bird.

GENERAL INFORMATION

Handling a sick bird requires skill and patience. Fright may intensify an already serious condition. Gentleness is the key word. The aforementioned symptoms and treatments are only general and if response is not noted, in the form of improvement, a veterinarian should be consulted.

There are times when it becomes necessary to put a bird out of his suffering. The owner must use his own judgment, but when he decides this action must be taken, the following is a simple, painless and sure process.

Attach a piece of cotton or gauze to the lid of a fruit jar or heavy cardboard box. Saturate the gauze thoroughly with chloroform. These quarters must be small enough so that the bird cannot move too freely. Place the bird in these confines and secure the lid tightly. Leave him there, without disturbing, for 30 minutes. Death will come without a struggle.